MIGHTY MACHINES

Taxis

by Kay Manolis

BELLWETHER MEDIA • MINNEAPOLIS, MN

Note to Librarians, Teachers, and Parents:

Blastoff! Readers are carefully developed by literacy experts and combine standards-based content with developmentally appropriate text.

Level 1 provides the most support through repetition of high-frequency words, light text, predictable sentence patterns, and strong visual support.

Level 2 offers early readers a bit more challenge through varied simple sentences, increased text load, and less repetition of high-frequency words.

Level 3 advances early-fluent readers toward fluency through increased text and concept load, less reliance on visuals, longer sentences, and more literary language.

Level 4 builds reading stamina by providing more text per page, increased use of punctuation, greater variation in sentence patterns, and increasingly challenging vocabulary.

Level 5 encourages children to move from "learning to read" to "reading to learn" by providing even more text, varied writing styles, and less familiar topics.

Whichever book is right for your reader, Blastoff! Readers are the perfect books to build confidence and encourage a love of reading that will last a lifetime!

This edition first published in 2009 by Bellwether Media.

No part of this publication may be reproduced in whole or in part without written permission of the publisher. For information regarding permission, write to Bellwether Media Inc., Attention: Permissions Department, Post Office Box 19349, Minneapolis, MN 55419.

Library of Congress Cataloging-in-Publication Data
Manolis, Kay.
  Taxis / by Kay Manolis.
    p. cm. — (Blastoff! readers. Mighty machines)
  Summary: "Simple text and full color photographs introduce young readers to taxis. Intended for students in kindergarten through third grade"—Provided by publisher.
  Includes bibliographical references and index.
  ISBN-13: 978-1-60014-232-1 (hardcover : alk. paper)
  ISBN-10: 1-60014-232-X (hardcover : alk. paper)
  1. Taxicabs—Juvenile literature. I. Title.
  TL232.5.M36 2009
  629.222'32—dc22   2008012235

Contents

Taxis are very helpful cars. They take people where they need to go.

A taxi has
a driver.

Passengers
sit in the back seat.

A taxi has a
roof light.
Taxi drivers
turn it
on when
they need
passengers.

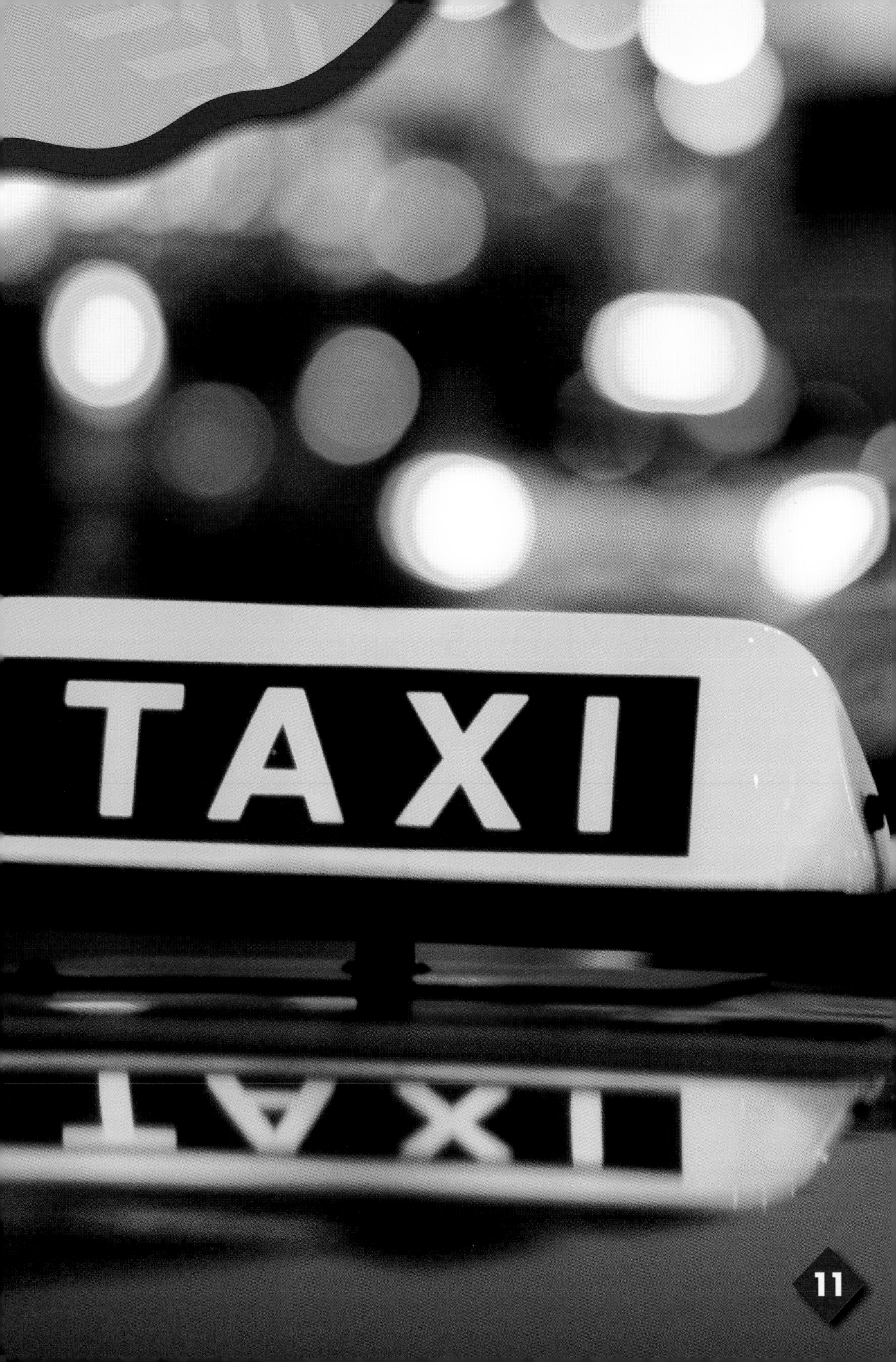
TAXI

This light is off. It means the taxi has passengers.

A taxi has a **meter**. It shows the cost of the ride.

$ EXTRAS

2.80

TIM

OFF   EXTRAS   RATE

centrodyne   RATE

Silent 610 ™

Made in Canada   Patent pending

S/N 49015

Some taxis drive around town. People wave to a taxi when they need a ride.

Some taxis stop at a **taxi stand**. The drivers wait for passengers.

These women need a ride to the airport. A taxi can do the job.

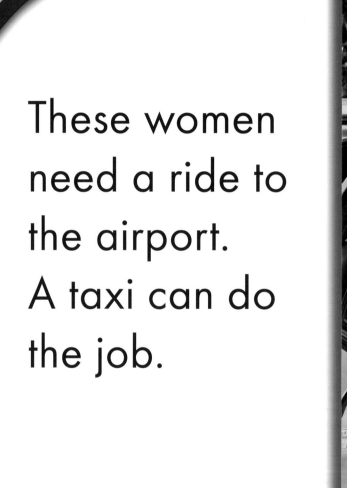

DRIVER CARRIE
ONLY $10.00 CHA

Glossary

meter—a machine that keeps track of the cost of a taxi ride

passengers—people who ride in a vehicle

taxi stand—a place where taxis stop and wait for people who need rides; most taxi stands are at airports and other busy places where many people need rides.

To Learn More

AT THE LIBRARY

Johnson, Stephen T. *My Little Yellow Taxi*. San Diego, Calif.: Harcourt, 2006.

Lassieur, Allison. *Taxis*. Minneapolis, Minn.: Bridgestone, 2000.

Wilson-Max, Ken. *Big Yellow Taxi*. New York: Scholastic, 1995.

ON THE WEB

Learning more about mighty machines is as easy as 1, 2, 3.

1. Go to www.factsurfer.com

2. Enter "mighty machines" into search box.

3. Click the "Surf" button and you will see a list of related web sites.

With factsurfer.com, finding more information is just a click away.

Index

The images in this book are reproduced through the courtesy of: emin kuliyev, front cover; Damir Spanic, p. 5; Altrendo Images / Getty Images, p. 7; Stephen Coburn, pp. 9, 21; allOver photography / Alamy, p. 11; Natalia Bratslavsky, p. 13; Raymond Forbes / age fotostock, p. 15; Getty Images, p. 17; WoodyStock / Alamy, p. 19.